"Hey Up There, I'm Down Here"

Book One

Tracking the Social Emotional Development of Infants and Toddlers

By C. L. Martin
Illustrated by: Stephen Adams

AuthorHouse™
1663 Liberty Drive
Bloomington, IN 47403
www.authorhouse.com
Phone: 1-800-839-8640

Published by AuthorHouse 05/07/2013

ISBN: 978-1-4817-4114-9 (sc)
         978-1-4817-5058-5 (e)

Library of Congress Control Number: 2013906855

This book is printed on acid-free paper.

authorHOUSE®

Introduction

This is Book One of a series of five books on the growth and development of infants and toddlers. This book provides information and insight into the social emotional development of infants and toddlers as seen through their eyes. Parents and all who read this book will laugh and maybe even cry (yes some of us are very sensitive) as they sit down and enjoy these fun filled fact- based children's books that you will want to read over and over again.

Children at any age can communicate weather it be through language, or other means of communication, so we have to look as well as listen to them to understand what they are trying to tell us.

If you see your child doing something that may surprise you or even stun you at whatever age send me an e-mail and I would love to explain what and why they are doing these things and what to expect next.

Joyandpain504@aol.com

About the Author

C.L. Martin, affectionately called "Kitty" by her family and friends and "Miss Kitty" by the thousands of children to whom she has been an educator for more than 30 years. Having some academic achievement in the area of Early Childhood Education, Miss. Kitty's wealth of knowledge and information stems mostly from hands on experience in the field of child care development and early childhood learning. It is her love for children, especially babies, that has inspired this book, the first in a series of five books of baby facts and fun. The parents of many of the children, to whom Miss Kitty has provided training, often seek her out for information and instruction. Children seem to respond to Miss Kitty more than to their parents in too many instances. Even her nephews and niece, Byron, Christopher, Charity and my daughter Tammy, to whom this book is dedicated, looked to Miss Kitty as a guardian and loved her deeply for the compassionate discipline she provided to them as toddlers.

Ask Miss Kitty what makes her so effective in working with children and she will tell you "it's because I can see through a child's eyes". Babies just want grown-ups to know that there is an unseen language that some parents don't grasp or understand. A lot of parents are unable to communicate with their children because they think above the child's level. This fun-filled book of facts is the voice of those little one's screaming "Hey! Up There, I'm Down Here!

Among other great accomplishments, Carrie has achieved her degree in Human and Social Service Management.

Social Emotional Relationships
Wrap Me Up!

"Ms. White, can you tell me why Charity gets so fussy when its time for her to take a nap? I have tried everything to make her feel comfortable and secure". Her diaper is dry and she has been fed; I don't understand! Take a small blanket and wrap her up snuggly with her little arms wrapped also."

"Hey up there, I like to feel like my mommy is right here with me, if you don't mind".

Fact: Almost from the time of birth (0-6 months) and sometimes older, like to be wrapped up by being "swaddled"-- a technical term used to give them a sense of being enclosed similar to the way they were in their mommies womb. So if your baby is fussy when its nap time or bed time, swaddle them. I almost guarantee, it will do the trick.

7

SOCIAL EMOTIONAL RELATIONSHIPS
"Do I Know These People"

"It is so amazing to me that when Aunt Sharon comes around, Charity seem to look around as if she knows that Sharon is in the room and, when Sharon goes to pick her up she has the biggest smile on her face as if she knew it was her picking her up and we know everybody can't pick Charity up and she smiles like that. "Oh please George she is only 3 months old how can she know Sharon came in the room, well she must like the way her aunt smells".

"Hey up there, I do know good perfume when I smell it."

Fact: At about the age of 3-4 months, babies start to recognize familiar voices, faces, and actually smells.

SOCIAL EMOTIONAL- RELATIONSHIPS
More, More, More, More, More!

"Denise why does Charity cry every time I stop singing to her, as if she knows what I am saying". George, Charity likes what she hears so if you cry when you can't have your ways what do you think about a baby".

"Hey up there, I can't sing it like you sing it but I like what I'm hearing and I want to hear more you got it".

Fact: When a babies is between the ages of 3-6 months hear sounds that are pleasant and familiar to them they have no idea what start and stop mean, all they know is they like what they hear and they want to hear more of it until they get bored or sleepy.

SOCIAL EMOTIONAL RELATIONSHIPS
I Have Eyes To see With!

"Miss Pat,can you believe that I was blinking my eye because something got in it and, I looked over at Alexander and he was doing the same thing back at me". "well something as simple as blinking your eyes is not very hard to do". "I know that but I didn't realize he was watching me ".

"Hey up there, if you noticed, I have eyes too and after all, I'm a big boy now".

Fact: babies will begin to notice more of their surroundings and will start to mimic behavior especially the social contact between themselves and other people that they are familiar with starting at around 6 months of age.

SOCIAL RELATIONSHIPS
Do You Think I Know You?

"Honey, have you noticed that every time Barbara visits, Charity starts to cry whenever she sees her? It makes me wonder? After all, Barbara is your sister.

"Hey up there, I don't see her enough to know who she is".

Fact: Children from the ages of five to fourteen months develop what is called "stranger anxiety" which speaks for itself. Children feel so uncomfortable around unfamiliar people (usually adults) they began to cry whenever they are present. This condition will usually stop at around fifteen months. So, if you are a relative or friend and you have experienced the "stranger anxiety" from a child, you know that it can make you feel really badly and very uncomfortable. Hey, it's not personal! It is a fact that children remember and recognize familiar faces.

Note: You can find more information on "stranger anxieties" at eHow.com.

SOCIAL EMOTIONAL-RELATIONSHIPS
I Am So Happy Now!

Miss Pat said, "Denise I left the classroom and came back, Charity must have heard me speaking to the teachers and all of a sudden she started crying and kicking hers feet and waving her hands, I didn't know what to make of it until when I picked her up she stopped crying and started smiling babbling".

"Hey up there yes I do love my teachers especially Miss Pat but, I love my mommy and daddy more.

Fact: Even though babies do have internal affections for their parents, they also develop attachments to other people especially their caregivers because, they spend a lot of quality time with these people.

SOCIAL EMOTIONAL RELATIONSHIPS
You Can Share With Me!

"George did you notice how Charity looked at you when you picked her up and you had that look of disgust on your face?" Well Denise, I guess she wanted to know what the problem was (laughing)."

"Hey up there, I might be small but I can hear and see too."

Fact: Babies can see, hear and actually feel the emotion of the people around them especially their parents and immediate caregivers. They can see the expression on your faces, they can hear the tone of your voices and they can feel the tension when you pick them up and hold them, so be very careful how you look, what you say and how you pick up the babies.

SOCIAL RELATIONSHIPS
"I Love You Too!"

"Denise, do you ever wonder when you drop Charity off at Day Care, why she immediately starts to look for Ms. Pat when she hears Miss Pat's voice and whenever she sees Miss Pat, she reaches out for her? "Well, maybe she thinks Miss Pat is her buddy.

"Hey up there, after all I do spend a lot of time with Miss Pat".

Fact: Children spend as little as four hours or as much as eleven hours in the care of someone other than their parents. Therefore, they form a very close bond with their caregiver, starting as early as 6 months. This can make some parents feel unwanted by the child. Of course, this is not true; however, the bond between the child and his/her caregiver and the bond between the child and his/her parent is two different relationships.

So, mommies and daddies just keep on loving your children and be thankful you have such wonderful caregivers taking care of your babies.

SOCIAL RELATIONSHIPS
"That Special Friend"

Miss Diane, have you noticed that during play time, Charity and Aiden always seem to find each other and then they start to play together".

"Hey up there we have friends too".

Fact: Children start to form relationships with other children at a very young age; usually around the age of six months. This relationship can grow into a friendship as long as they have contact with each other.

SOCIAL EMOTIONAL RELATIONSHIPS
If You Can Do It, I Can Too!

"George do you know I licked out my tongue at Charity and can you believe she did the same thing back at me". "Well George something as simple as licking out your tongue at someone, how silly".

"Hey up there, if you can make those funny faces at me well, back at you, after all I'm a big girl now".

Fact: babies will begin to notice more of their surroundings and will start to mimic behavior especially the social contact between themselves and other people that they are familiar with starting at around 6 months of age.

SOCIAL RELATIONSHIPS
I Think That Is My Man

"Miss Hunter, I thought Aiden and Charity were buddies but, look at Aiden and Isabella. Oh I think they still are,look at Charity pushing Alexandra out of the way, I'd better stop them.

"Hey up there, so Ben cheated on me, I'm over it and I want my man back."

Fact: Children do form relationships ships with other children as young as 6-7 months of age. They do play with other children but, they tend to gravitate towards favorite children and actually become very aggressive when their favorite buddy interact with other kids.

SOCIAL EMOTIONAL-RELATIONSHIPS
Playing Chasing Games

"While I was playing with Charity, I crawled around the table a couple of times and Charity got on her knees and began to chase after me, it was so funny and if I stopped she would stop."

"If my daddy only knew, it doesn't take much to catch him after all he is so old."

Fact: As children grow and become more mobile, they move around more then, they start to mimic what they see others do and with great detail. They may even start initiating things they have done before that they enjoyed doing. As they grow they are able to imitate more skills.

Note: Even though this skill is included in this book it can also be included in my book on movement".

SOCIAL RELATIONSHIPS
Stranger No More

"Denise, did you noticed when I came into the room that Charity didn't cry. Barbara, I think she is becoming comfortable with you around her now.

"Hey I'm a big girl now and besides she is family and I cant avoid her forever.

Fact: The condition called "stranger anxiety" usually starts to go away about the age of 14 months but, it can vary depending on the child because, every child is different.

SOCIAL RELATIONSHIPS
Well let Everybody Sing

Lien started to cry when her mom left the center. then Isabella crawled across the floor, and she started to cry too. while the kids were having free play, Cameron started crying because he was hungry for his snack. Danielle was sitting and playing with some toys and she started to cry as well.

"Hey up there, we have feeling for each other after all, we spend more time together than with anybody else."

Fact: Of course it is emotional, when children hear /see other children cry usually around the age of 14 months, they may already be in a bad mood, maybe missing their parents or any other reason to cry they do.

SOCIAL RELATIONSHIPS
Seeking Companionship

While the children were havin free play, Hanna was trying to stack some blocks when, Charity sat down beside her and started to do the same thing.

"She looked like she was having so much fun sitting there doing her thing I wanted to do her thing too."

Fact: Children are pretty much loners up to the age of about 14 months, then they will start to engage in play with other children and develop favoritism towards them. At around 18 or 20 months moths, they tend to mimic what they see other children do as well as other people so, it is very important that we as parents and caregivers watch what we do and say around them, in order for them to pick up the good habits.

SOCIAL RELATIONSHIPS
Can't You See I'm Having a Problem

While playing on the blanket at playtime, Charity suddenly stiffened her body up and began to cry when she rolled off the blanket and on the grass.

"Sometime, the only way I can get attention is when I roll over and play dead."

Fact: Usually between the ages of 18-24 months, children will start to display this behavior. It could be in fits of anger, crying, screaming kicking, falling down and stiffening of their limbs.

Note: I have actually seen babies as young as 5 months have tantrums so, again it depends on the child.

SOCIAL RELATIONSHIPS
I Guess I Have To Comfort Myself

I noticed when Jordan (Charity's cousin) was playing with the truck and Charity walked over to him and snatched it away from him, Bing then walked over to his teacher and sat on her lap.

"When I see something I want, I just take it, remember, I am just a kid."

Fact: When children are at the age between the ages of 18-24 months, they tend to become aggressive and possessive. Some don't like to use the word aggressive but, because their vocabulary is limited they act out their frustrations.

Printed in the United States
by Baker & Taylor Publisher Services